CW01512798

Nottingham PHILIP CALLOW UNITED

NOTTINGHAM IS MY SECOND HOME, where I had a second birth. Every time I go there, the past hits me. The hour of birth coming on, the struggle, the sad and the glad ghosts. Ghosts everywhere. Even D. H. Lawrence, glowering through the fog, rancorous, his hate killing him. " There is no Nottingham " he wrote, a year before he died. What he meant was, to make a city you have to unite, make a big gesture, be a citizen.

Every time I go there. I get out at Nottingham Midland and start to lug a suitcase all the way into town; past Woolworths, up the narrow arcade by St. Peter's into Slab Square. I gorge on the past, chew the cud of old experiences, every step of the way. It's automatic. A Mapperly bus swings me round by the theatre and down Sherwood Street, past the library, the fire-station. Ghosts. memories. Mansfield Road, the past billowing and thick and murky, so dense, as we turn into Woodborough Road, that I can hardly see the houses.

Once it was the past and nothing else. That's terrible. Now it's more, much more, and I don't know how it's happened, but how glad I am. Nottingham unites things for me, more than any other place. Unites things inside me. I am alienated no longer. The physical Nottingham I still find as gruesome as ever, like my own birthplace, Birmingham, like Manchester, like Coventry where I grew up. If these industrial rat-traps with their miles of charred terraces, miles of nasty little homes, could be razed to the ground without hurting a hair of anybody's head, I'd say: quick, do it. Press the button! I hope I never have an uglier journey to work than my daily trip to the Ordnance

PHILIP CALLOW comes from Coventry, but is Nottingham· by marriage. He is the author of Common People *1958,* Native Ground *1959,* A Pledge for the Earth *1960, and of the TV play* The Honeymooners.

Factory, for instance, during my three months sentence. Round by the dance hall, the Labour Exchange, a sharp left turn along Wilford Road, away from that castle and its rock wallowing in the streets, black, like a bull, the view worsening steadily as you drew nearer the factory gates. Then you really abandoned hope. Leaving at night the back way, alongside North Shop and out over the railway tracks to Lenton, in a landscape devastated like a battlefield, I used to feel like a convict, really one of the living dead, on the run from a chain gang. No wonder I grabbed at love, no wonder I hung on, no wonder I begged and struggled to be born.

Nottingham, thank God, is also people, Nottingham unites me now with Birmingham, Coventry and Plymouth, with Kingston, Calcutta and Karachi, and the result, strangely enough, is not a monster. It is a world of people. People who come and go as I do, people who stay, live and die, give birth, people who are arriving immigrants. The people are a mystery, they change all the time. In 1950 I go to Nottingham to live, so as to be near a woman who is virtually giving birth to me—my second birth. But she doesn't finish it, and anyway you have to die first. She was also killing me. I died more than once, had more than one rebirth. I meet a group of young anarchists, adrift like myself, and all this time in Nottingham—nine months!—I am living my first book, though I have to go away and wait years to write it. And how it makes me suffer. Meanwhile, another woman takes hold of me, this one really in earnest, and she drags me bodily into new life, in Nottingham.

Things have a way of happening to me in Nottingham. I see *Sum Total* in a bookshop window and think no more of it. But it works away, ferments, and I end up knocking on the author's door. This writer tells me nothing about the city. He takes me to a pub, I sit listening to scraps of conversation, see him mixing with the locals, hear arguments about the police, a bus strike, and the whole place takes on a new dimension. My father-in-law, an old man of eighty, brings the old days to life, the old town, the pubs, the outlying villages—I hear it from his lips as I once read it in the pages of Lawrence. Outside in the street the new immigrants go up and down, move into houses opposite, come off the transport shifts. West Indians, Indians, Pakistanis. They are another new dimension. They aren't accepted, only tolerated, and doubtless they don't accept us either, or even each other. But they must, and we must—or history will drag us back, kill us with the past. They are here, and that is a fact which alters everything. Equal in Nottingham. Every time I pass one I say welcome, welcome under my breath. Give us time to change. Let us live together for a few years, a few decades, a few centuries. Let the children decide, for themselves, what we can never decide. Unite, or stay separate. Be a citizen, or hide away in a little home.

Nottingham, to paraphrase James Baldwin, is white no more. And it will never be white again. The world is now coming into this Nottingham which Lawrence wanted pulled down to the last brick, for " an absolute clean start ". This is the next best thing. Or maybe, for all we know, it is even better.

ROBIN HOOD RIDES AGAIN
-a rebel scene: - RAY•GOSLING

I CAME TO NOTTINGHAM because I was running away from Leicester. Didn't fancy living in the south of England. Didn't fancy the North. I wanted to be near to Leicester but in a big city, and so this place—Queen of the Midlands, Arse of the North—I thought would suit me well. By train it is only two hours from London, St. Pancras.

Wanted to be anonymous. Came to this city and hoped I could live here without having to shout out from the rooftops. I wanted no-one to know my name. At first I was successful. It covered me like a cosy wrap blanket. Greater Nottingham with its suburbs holds nearly a million people. Townland runs west into Derby and north all the way to Sheffield. It is large and civilised—first division football. You can eat well, two theatres, film spectaculars, night clubs: yet it has no " town life ". The coffee bar set move from the Kardomah to the Don Juan with their cars and their girls in a self-contained world. Radford has its own. Bulwell. The Meadows. The rich. The lesbian. The mod. The folk music fadder—and these worlds meet rarely which would be alright if we were really big, but this is a second division city—out of the Manchester, Liverpool, Glasgow, Birmingham class.

The University, stuck out on a hill lies fat and lush and large in its self-important pomposity and never comes to the town.

I knew no-one when I first came and didn't want to. I could nod to people on the street, in the shops and on nights out around the town with people and we learnt nothing about each other but our Christian names: often never met again.

I knew that CND held meetings on the Old Market Square on Sundays—like the Salvation Army and the Pentecostals and the Communist Party, they arrived, set themselves up, spoke, answered questions, chatted, and then left in their groups to their own halls and boozers and lives. It was all like watching Variety from the front stalls at the Theatre Royal.

Been here some time and set up a home, the first proper home I've ever had—a flat, but still a home: two bedrooms, front room, hot and cold, immersion heater, bathroom, kitchen, corridor—comfortable and fully furnished at £5. 5. a week and have to pay for your own electricity which is why I am now writing this by candlelight. And yet because there is a back boiler I am able to shave, and wash and bath; opposite Players cigarette factory and two streets up from Old Radford parish

RAY GOSLING, born in Northampton, read English for one year at University of Leicester and left to help operate the West End Coffee Bar, a cafe and dance hall and club run by the Townies for the Townies. Now lives in Nottingham. Wrote Lady Albermarle's Boys (1961) *and* Sum Total (1962). *Recently made a BBCtv film* Two Town Mad *about Leicester and Nottingham, and is at present working on an* Urban Ramble Round Britain, *to be published by Faber at the end of the year.*

church.

It would be more than a year of Nottingham when I went to a New Left weekend school at Burley in Wharfedale. On the diesel coming out from Leeds, looking at every station to see the nameboard; an edgy, nervous journey, making notes—what am I going to say ?—what station's that ?—how much further ? I hate John Rex—and looking over on the other side of the gangway was another man with a briefcase also making notes. Think nothing of it. The train thins of passengers and is most commuterless by, at last, Burley in Wharfedale. I got off. He got off, and as the ticket collector took the outgoing half of our return tickets we look at each other. Shy. Speak—new left—yes—ah yes and so am I—and we walk together, suspicions proved right, smugly, up the muddy path to the house and that was how I met Ken Coates of Nottingham.

Today, Ken Coates, native of Sussex, ex-Derbyshire pit-man is vice-chairman of the city Labour Party, lecturer in adult education for the University, a founder of UNION VOICE, the monthly trade union sheet; co-editor with Robin Blackburn of THE WEEK, digest of news for busy socialists; and British co-editor with Jim Mortimer of the INTER-NATIONAL SOCIALIST JOURNAL—healthy triplets all started during last year. It is not that they are exciting, amusing, highly significant or even fabulously alive. They are more like fertiliser: essential.

In the house where Brother Coates lived then, downstairs was the landlord, Mr. Peter Price. Now, anyone writing for a living who is stubborn and pig headed enough to choose to live outside London must put up with, or so the legend runs, and isn't part of all legend true—agonies of isolation, seizures of dull cramp, lethargy, boredom and final extinction. To enter their house, to enter " 54 " was to enter a world of candlelight, wood fires, and Wagner loud on the record player and it either repulsed you or as it did for me, fascinated, lifted the leeches from beneath the eyes. It was a meeting ground, a talking shop and all sorts from all parts would come in and go out through the same door, with much the same opinions as they went in with—as you do when you go to chapel—only you'd been strengthened. 54 was a powerhouse, and still is, a hive of rebels and none of them a rascal; the antipodes of " 110 "; the Labour Party headquarters on Mansfield Road. In the same planet but the other side.

The virtue of the 54 network was I think that it was a network, and not a club or a cell. Solidarity was a word often used and rarely applied. It was people, certain politically active, conscious people from CND; from the young socialists; once communist cadres; it was Ken the rose gardener; John and Edward the university academics; Rod the carpet salesman; miner, student, engineer. The fault was in that it was easy enough and the battles hard enough to make it self-perpetuating, the re-telling of tales—the love of its own rituals, language, manners—the danger of pride in the signs.

CND, as an experiment wanted to launch on a large scale a publicity campaign using newspapers, billboards, leaflets, advertising galore; and as a pilot scheme they settled on Greater Nottingham. After the campaign a public meeting was held in the Co-op Arts Centre for which a large audience turned up. Several television, only faintly remembered, personalities spoke and the platform kept apologising for the absence of much advertised film actor Stanley Baker. After that, there was a nice sherry and thinner than cut slice sandwich do at the George Hotel for the local and national campaigners to get together. (There was a similar do for the Kenya Independance Day celebrations laid on by the Kenya Government who seem to have so much money to throw about, that I've thought of asking them to pay my electric bill). After the do, the two professionals who has more or less tagged along so far (George Clark and Stuart Hall) were transported to beer and loud talk by those on the 54 network. It was near dawn and cold when after argument, anger, dissension, rage, walk-out, drunkenness and chaos two tired national campaigners gave Nottingham up to its own confusion.

Before I discovered this underworld of action and revolution, inspired by the Slab Square meetings I did, four or five times, go to the Friends' Meeting House to hear the voices for a unilateral policy and in the new Swedish light and polished wood room, before the thick and small china cups of coffee came round the Quakers would hold forth, respectable, sensible and tame. During questions the raughters made attempts at breaking down the restraint.

The next I knew of CND was on the 54 network, from where the kernel of marshals and organisers and secretaries and committees were now being formed, fixed and activated.

All I know now of the campaign is in circular letters from the satellite town of Beeston which are kind and uninspiring and none ever read. The Sunday meetings on the square have gone. But forms and things are sent to my place from YCND in London inviting me to conferences, asking me to follow up a new member on this or that housing estate—the confusion and muddle which has card indexed my place as the local secretariat is a little beyond me. The best thing the national campaign at Carthusian Street can do seems to me to forget that CND in this city exists and wait until some fresh spirit starts the argument up again on another wavelength. The same, all through this more or less applies to the Committee of 100.

When Centre 42 arrived here last year they opened the week's programme on the Sunday with poetry and jazz only to find that their day and their time corresponded exactly with that of the Playhouse Theatre poetry and jazz evening. Saboteurs, said Centre 42—Foreigners said the Playhouse. The local artists and Centre 42 became so locked in argument that the pictures in pubs project didn't come off. Co-operation where it existed at all was between Arnold Wesker and Company and the Trades Council as an official body. People never got together. It was not surprising that only a handful turned up to see and hear the bits and pieces of the Festival. It was a miracle anyone did. This city is a proud city. It is the regional capital of the East Midlands. It is large enough to be Greater, but small enough NOT to be metropolitan: a pompous minded, brassy, almost Yorkshire kind of town. It is no use Wesker complaining at the apathy of the workers, and the inconsideration of the Co-op hall management as he did a month or so ago when he held a return poetry and jazz session to a dozen people in a hall above the room where the Broast Street Beat Club where having a Rave Night. It is sad they didn't find out beforehand. It is sad that they have about them the airs of supercilious crusaders, come to save a city that has got to save itself, if at all.

At 4 Fletcher Gate, above Julian's restaurant, clean and cheap and chic and angled for the lunch time trade, in the Lace Market, the city's equivalent of the Birmingham jewellery quarter, a kind of miniature City of London is the Communist Party. They usually put up three or four candidates in the local elections and one at the general and do quite well. They are alive and not as much Friends of the Soviet Philharmonic as others tend to be. They publish sheets and handouts and pamphlets from time to time and John Peck, the secretary wrote a pamphlet price sixpence—NOTTINGHAM FOR YOU—the best analysis, if a little out of date now in its details, more to the point and accurate and telling than anything else written on the city today that I've come across:

> "The Tories who tried to scrap our Civic Theatre are the direct political descendants of those who opposed the opening of Nottingham's first public library in 1868, on the grounds that reading would be dangerous to the contentment of their workers."

The political scene is jumping here just as the flower beds on the traffic islands are splendid and colourful; very fine, uplifting: makes your morning eyes feel glad. The New Left Club brings in people from the corners of the world to speak beneath the fluorescent brightness of the Mechanics Institute. There is the famed Jordan's International Bookstore for all your socialist literature—tucked away in a back street, hidden behind a front of second hand paper backs, thrillers and all, gad what, Comrade.

And the Young Fabians—set up only eighteen months ago have produced three pamphlets. Not with the punch of the Communist document these are a little more learned—POLITICAL ISSUES IN NOTTING-HAM,—A HOUSING PLAN FOR NOTTINNGHAM (there are 40,000 obsolescent houses,)—PRIVATE SCHOOLS IN NOTTINGHAM.

True to Fabian traditions they decided to hold a day school for Labour candidates and councillors some time before the '63 May elections. Being mostly at the university they offered their brains to be picked by the future city council—the day was well prepared and the councillors and candidates thought such a refresher course would be good for them, all eager beaver and keen and on the day only one Labour candidate turned up, and none of the councillors.

It is not that this now controlled by the Labour Group city council is composed of evil men. More likely it is tired minds. Flower beds are lovely oases. Flower beds are like closed clubs. Our city fathers fear more than God attempting anything grand enough, so adventurous that it might excite the people, that it might change the city.

On a wet night in December The Beatles came to the Odeon. The following night Lord Snowden with the Lord Mayor and the Vice Chancellor of the University, and the Duke of Portland and others (Princess Margaret couldn't come because she was having a baby and so sent her regrets with her husband): all came to see open at last the plush civic theatre and be tickled a little with *Coriolanus*. (Excerpts only because the speeches took so long.)

I had thought of making a protest—what a way to open such a beautiful building; what a way to open a theatre whose birth had been such a comic opera of party political in-fighting—why not fireworks, revue and bunny-girls and general rejoicing—why not like The Beatles the night before—why not like Harry Worth who came at the end of that week to be ready to star in pantomime. A camera, oh for a camera to be trained one day on the box office at the New Playhouse and the next at the Harry Worth. What comedy and tragedy would be in those pictures, only they were never taken. And I did nothing about the opening of the theatre because I couldn't get that worked up about the idea, and there wasn't that much money, and after all it wasn't fair to protest when after such a battle the theatre was actually open. After all John Neville had given up life in London as a star to come here and be the sun and the moon of just one Solar system—so we stood and watched; stood in the small crowd of women who clapped and cheered timidly as Snowden ran for his car. Next day read in the papers of how the actors arrived at the civic reception at the council house to find no food, and the Mayor said go in there and they went towards the door, and the Town Clerk blocked the way, and then there was a punch up; and the day after that the council were demanding an apology from the New Playhouse and the New Playhouse were demanding an apology from the council house. The row has now subsided and the theatre plays on directed by the triumvir of John Neville, Frank Dunlop and Peter Ustinov. It saves you the two pound return rail fare to Shaftesbury Avenue. Like it is another flower bed, you catch a glimpse of it from the top of the bus and think how lovely and long to plant marihuana between the daffodils—because it isn't a theatre of the people not even as much as the other place is where Harry Worth closed after two months of packed houses of Dick Whittington.

Little wonder that in such an atmosphere you shed a tear and keep firm on your own network.

The city's Pigalle Club advert in the paper:— " Owing to public demand we announce a complete change of programme next week." There have been good happenings like that—down by Trentside a whole jazz complex has mushroomed in the past two years into a really lively scene. The fleapit Scala has been taken over by the Classic Cinema chain. The folk workshop, sadly set in the liquorless Co-op Arts Centre blossoms and a monthly magazine of suburban short stories and bric brac NOTTINGHAM PARADE, a kind of local Readers' Digest flourishes. The Midland Artists' Group Gallery opposite the New Playhouse has become a main-shows-always-reviewed-in THE GUARDIAN art gallery without losing the basement which can be hired by almost anyone; cheap and worthwhile and noticed.

One night last April I sat in the Ghost Pub and the 54 crowd were in and the municipal elections pending and people were talking and saying how Peter was a good man and would be good for the council, only the city labour party seem to operate a mild-Macarthy policy—reserving special wards for the bright, new-blood and willing yet not in on their " 110 " official Labour Party Club/Network—wards, all of them with large Tory majorities.

But, people said, the swing is to Labour and this Lenton Ward could be marginal. If only Liberal would stand and split the vote then Peter might stand some chance. If only one of us were not so involved and caught up in the local Labour Party one of us could stand. If only. And in my pots I stood up and boasted how I would stand and split the vote and make the difference. The laughs around me were loud and chilling. Walking around the area in the normal course of a day's business and pleasure people said—good idea—you ought to stand—needs shaking up, will you be Labour?—look at this and they call themselves a council—you'll have my vote. I had been lumbered. The week came for the nominations. It was a question of pride and honour. I had to stand—no it wasn't only that. For two years living as a passive citizen in this listless city and never showed at all what I felt. I sat down and wrote out a manifesto and every word I meant:

VOTE FOR A MADMAN. JUST FOR ONCE IN YOUR LIFE. VOTE FOR A MADMAN. I am not a politician. I am not your "honest candidate." I have no support from any political party. But please read on.

I am a not rich, 23-year-old professional freelance scribbler (writer) who settled eighteen months ago on Hartley Road, Radford—and I'm asking you, electors of Lenton, to make me your REPRESENTATIVE on Nottingham City Council.

On May 9th, I would like You to vote for Me—Independent Liberal.

Where's my interest ? Why am I doing this ? I tell you I'm doing this for FUN, and for LOVE—for love of this Nottingham, city of nearly one million people with its suburbs and outskirts—a great city that I am proud to live in, very very proud—so proud that now as a citizen I am not prepared to go to the Poll and cast a vote for the shower of crumbling, muddle-headed and funked-up councillors of a city that seems to an outsider to be falling asleep and slowly into chaos while grown men fight among themselves in that Council House at Slab Square.

I can't keep still or silent, merely voting when the state of this city I've made my home shames me so much—not that it is bad—but because it could be SO GOOD: and it isn't, while I have energy, and can make time, and as we live in a supposedly Democratic country, I offer myself to you, the people of Lenton.

Electors of Nottingham—wake up—travel to Leicester, Coventry, Birmingham and see new buildings rising up, cities moving forward, modern and active ; living and growing richer in every way—come back to this, by tradition, the Queen of the Midlands—one of the richest, most advanced and civilised areas in the world and you see a shambles where it shouldn't be—a city ripe and ready to develop and move into the 1960's, but swimming in its own slime ; shambling along in the 1950's without imagination, guts or go.

It is easy for a city to become tatty and then a second rate place. Too many promises have been made by our councillors, and too few have been kept. Maybe there are reasons, but I would like to know them.

And I stand for Lenton Ward, because to someone who comes from outside it is a very special ward, having what must be Nottingham's three most famous areas :-

RADFORD
. . . where "Saturday Night and Sunday Morning" has made the 58 bus route world-renowned : for the laughter, and the pubs, and the finest girls in England—those Players Dollies.

THE MEADOWS
. . . I was fifteen and never been here, when I first heard of the houses off Wilford Road, a boy at school I was told of the slums, the bad housing that still exist in 1963 — The Meadows.

and THE PARK Estate
. . . busless, shopless, exclusive and private — You can walk from the

Castle to Park Road on an afternoon and not pass one single person.
LENTON WARD
Lenton is a very special Ward. I wouldn't want to change its character, in
either The Park or the other side of Derby Road—but the roads in The
Park are falling apart ; too many houses outside there still have no lavatory
and no bathroom.
Lenton is somewhere special—special enough I feel to send to the Council
for one term of three years a man with—

> NO POLICY
> NO PROGRAMME
> and NO FEAR

I have nothing to lose, no reputation, no business, no property—and I can
afford to say just what I please. A Council wouldn't work at all with many
madmen—but without one or two fearless little men it can get too big for its
boots and DIE.
When the Labour Group ran the Council they promised and promised and
promised this and that and the other—and along came the scandal of Popkess
and the Planetarium. And then came power to the Tory Group who promise
and promise and came the scandal of the Civic Theatre—and now more
promises.
I can promise little but to act as a catalyst, to shake-up the others, to
ginger-up their promises—into facts. To try to find out why it seems to
take so many years for a Council to keep its word.
I want you to vote for a madman, who if elected can have no loyalty but to
Lenton Ward, and my own love of this city.
CHANCE IT—Chance an Independent Liberal—and I promise one thing,
firmly, if after SIX MONTHS I have had no effect—and as I wander around
your ward in your pubs, and shops, and in your homes and on your streets you
tell me so—then I shall resign. That I do say.
On Thursday, 9th May you have a choice—

> Tory promises and Sanity ! !
> Labour promises and Sanity ! !

. . or a Freeman and a Voice that won't keep silent—

Say no more. I believe that. Try it yourself. You need no
deposit. I found a copy of the Labour Party booklet on local elections.
For three weeks this was my Bible, my chart through the oceans of red
tape and ceremony. An agent, and we were on. Wandered through
those I knew well in the ward (you must choose a ward where you are
known fairly well)—parents of friends and others—many signed—there
were completed nomination papers. It is only necessary to have one
with twelve signatures, but even with more I still hadn't a properly
signed paper. At the Town Clerk's office where I found a nice young
lady who helped me. Showed me where I was wrong. Back to the
ward. Try again. Made it. To her superior. To the Town Clerk.
Signed and sealed and it was all in order this time. I was duly nomin-
ated : candidate for Lenton Ward, Independant Liberal. I still thought,
then, that I might with this tag take some Liberal votes. Terrified of
polling two figures.

The evening papers spread it a little—" Last minute surprise nomination "—and the next day I was invaded by the Liberal Party. At first
they were persuasive. Then puzzled. Finally they left convinced—I
was not a Liberal.

I held a press conference, and the papers printed chunks of manifesto. Out in the ward nippers squealing after me—here comes the
madman mam—many people will have to try this type of campaign
before it is accepted that not only do we have a vote for the Council,

but we can stand. Politics everyone thought was power, and where was my power—the days had passed of the little men. The ward was buzzing. We ran a full-blooded, disorganised campaign—toured the boozers—every house had a manifesto and visited many—with no money and no experience and a handful of enthusiastic, half-giggled workers, many of whom were too young to vote, we felt good.

The great day came—the moment of truth. That morning's Manchester GUARDIAN carried a feature headed " Like Mad "—a journalist had spent a night with the campaign—Killed were any last hopes of kidding anyone I was anything but an unaligned stirrer-up. The Liberal Club had already barred me as an imposter. Up early and trudging the streets. The Tory cavalcades were out in force. The Labour Party were roving in cars and vans and I was catching the bus. We did have people stuck by the polling booths but we had no idea how many votes we were catching, or where they were coming from. At six I retired in defeat. At seven we had an army of supporters. They lifted us all dayers into a revival with two cars and one van. Optimism. Back round the houses and at nine it was over. At eleven the results were out.

J. Gough (con.)	2,511	53%
P. Price (lab.)	1,687	36%
R. Gosling (ind.)	475	11%

There had been a poll of 41% of the electorate. The campaign had cost £36. The Tory made his victory speech, clean fight, best man winning. The Labour candidate, his thank you mister returning officer and all, clean fight and then the eyes in the counting room turned towards our table. I couldn't face it. We rose and walked out, bad losers.

Was it worth it all ? Yes: a worthwhile spanner thrown at the people-matter-like-machines camps, and a giggle, and good stories to tell. I'm not sure about a parliamentary election. They need a lot of money and where the candidates as Lord Sutch at Stratford and William Rushton in West Perth and Kinross are not local living men there's not much chance. Both of those polled under 0% which must have broken a tear duct or two. Local elections: yes.

And next year ? Not like that anyway because never do a straight good repeat. It would be alright to do it if during the past year we had built up a fairly organised force to make a real stab at getting onto the council. I couldn't do this because I'm not sure now if I'll be here for three years more. One idea is to have a " mad man " candidate standing in each ward of the city, every one. That could have some effect, but there again it needs fabulous promotion. Another idea that needs fabulous money as well as promotion would be to run a campaign saying vote for no-one: spoil your ballot papers by marking them bullshit, andy capp, or some slogan—so that the returning officers, the candidates and their agents, party officials would have a shock. The point of all this ?

As we have the vote and it was fought hard for it is a complete waste I believe to abstain. There is often, as in Nottingham little point in voting for either party because they are both very much thick and

thicker. To write " goodbye " on your ballot paper having taken the
trouble to use your vote, however negatively is a way of showing active
disapproval in the ballot box.

Nottingham is small enough not to be like Mc., Lpool., Bham—
filled with—well take football—Everton and Liverpool: Aston Villa and
Birmingham City: Manchester United and City: Rangers and Celtic—
Nottingham doesn't have this metropolitan atmosphere. Yet it is large
enough not to have a " town " loyalty and " town " life that goes with
Leicester, Wolverhampton, Derby, Burnley, Coventry, Peterborough.
It is Greater and not Metropolitan. Football loyalties are divided
between Forest in Division One and County in Division Three—and
there is not much cohesive all town loyalty to either. The support is
divided, and so the city life. It works on networks, rather than gangs
or clubs and in spite of having a fine city centre there is no central focus
for the whole townspeople.

This may be partly because the press in Nottingham—the morning
GUARDIAN JOURNAL and the evening EVENING POST, both owned locally
are unbelievably unimaginative and often vile. I haven't written about
work very much because of space—but the main employers: Boots,
paternatistic: Players the same and Raleigh, now owned by Tube
Investments have become real bastards.

Recently the troubles at Raleigh came to a head, and the toolmakers
came out on strike. This meant that many others had to be laid off.
The usual story. The local papers have presented so one sided a story
of this that they ought to be reported to the Press Council for their
conduct. Headlines were made from a group of housewives, led by a
lady from Eastwood where D. H. Lawrence was born, who were per-
suaded into forming an anti-strike committee to get their husbands most
of whom were laid off and not on strike, back at work whatever the
cost. They have basked in print and glory—and the strikers and the
unions have received all shares of the blame. The whole issue is com-
plicated by in-fighting inside the unions and between the unions and
the men, which has so far been kept reasonably quiet. But love that
front page of the NOTTINGHAM EVENING POST one night to print what a
striker said to me, and he wasn't an active union man—Raleigh don't
want to make bicycles. They want to do contract work for the motor
industry. They want women and youths. They want to cut down
expenses and give the shareholders bigger profits—in the year before
Tube Investments took them over Raleigh declared a profit of over
£2 millions—yet they could sell bicycles all over the world, in Latin
America and Africa and Asia. Japan can do it. There is long term
money in it, but Raleigh want profits NOW. To sell over the world
needs hard selling. It needs the bosses to roll up their sleeves and
sweat their way through Asia and spend hours with governments and
accountants working out proper credit facilities for the buyers. Hard
work, and they don't want it. Easier to slowly turn the factory over
to the small stuff and employ women and children and they can sell the
bits and bobs easy in Birmingham and Coventry. Little work and fat
profits now, and the men—laid off. That is part of the Raleigh story.

One idea of my own is—and if anyone reading this thinks it good enough to work on, and thinks I could help then I'm game. Be marvellous to see a paper set up in the city for the city and by the city. Not necessarily appearing every week or fortnight or month. Maybe arriving only now and then when something special happened like the Raleigh strike or the opening of the New Playhouse, or municipal elections. A paper that is a kind of fifth column, an ombudsman—a cross between the Nick Luard SCENE and ANARCHY and PRIVATE EYE and the 1960 NEW LEFT REVIEW and TOWN and WHAT'S ON IN LONDON GUIDE —only based and rooted in this city. Being in part a local news digest with comment. In part a guide to the scene in Greater Nottingham: where to eat, what jazz is where, what club is doing what from The Stork to Amateur Theatre and the Miners Welfares. In part a voice of the people—reporting on what happens by the people it happens to, like the man from Raleigh, like the Vox Pop programmes the BBC puts out in some regions. Using tape-recorders for this, and then printing it out. And the fourth part a place for local poems and short stories and cartoons.

Something to be an umbrella to the networks and not another network. The present newspaper combine is not a network. It is more of a closed club and a secret society. A paper might work better than a building. The Co-op Arts Centre is good, but there are no bars and corridors and places where you can just wander. You go there as to most other " Centres " in the city for a purpose.

One last splendid idea that has arisen to thrill me in the last few weeks is from the Students' Union at the University who are thinking of building a Students' Union type of building in the heart of the city— for all of us, students and non-students—with bars and rooms and corridors. It could be exciting. It could even happen.

This town is jumping out all over, but like self-contained cells or the flower beds on the traffic islands—Most of the time you don't know what the other pieces are jumping around with—nor they you—and Nottingham isn't London. Not even metropolitan. The scene here is only alive when you know where.

from the Nottingham EVENING POST—Thursday 27 February 64

Mr. David Turner of Boundary Road, West Bridgford, said last night he was "hoisted to his feet" by a steward at the meeting on Monday in the Albert Hall, Nottingham, which was addressed by Mr. Edward Heath.

And last night, Mr. J. D. Crosland, chairman of the Nottingham Conservative Federation, who organised the meeting, said he would make the fullest investigation. "If indeed anyone was hoisted to his feet I shall ask that an apology be made," he stated.

Earlier, Mr. Turner, who was wearing a CND badge on his lapel, said: "I am not an anarchist, but I simply do not agree with having to stand every time this tune is played. I do not consider it a fitting National Anthem."

Mr. Turner was sitting with five friends during the meeting. As the Anthem was played he and his colleagues remained seated. "The next thing I knew was that a steward had grasped me by the jacket from behind and pulled me to my feet," he said.

He alleges that he was held there until the music stopped.

One of the stewards who was present on Monday night said that he considered it discourteous to remain seated during the playing of the National Anthem.

NOTTINGHAM AT 14

. . . when you seen Nottingham Castle and Wollaton Park you seen about the lot. *C.B.*

Nottingham is a city with a history that reaches back at least to the early days of the Anglo Saxons and today presents a picture of open boulevards and ancient thoroughfares, lovely parks and a great amount of industry. . . . *P.B.*

I my self would prefer to live some where els. *S.C.*

Nottingham is said to have been founded very early on about 450 AD by a man called Snot who brought his family to settle here. They first called the town Snottingham but as time went by people found that they did not like this name for their town so they changed it to Nottingham.

There is not very much night life in Nottingham which is one of the criticisms that I have of it. Nottingham has its fair share of cinemas but the other interests of younger people are left uncatered for. On the whole Nottingham is quite a good place to live in but if I had the chance to live in a smaller, more modern town I would certainly accept it. *A.B.*

The "City of Smoke was once mentioned to me in respect of Nottingham. I am entitled to agree. *P.E.*

Nottingham is one of the cleanest cities I have seen. Sheffield, Leeds, Liverpool, Manchester and Glasgow seem to me dirty compared to Nottingham . . . The Council House, I think, is one of the most attractive in England, other Council Houses seem always to be dingy and dirty looking. *I.G.*

I have lived in Nottingham for about 3 years and before that in Newark which is in Nottinghamshire. I have watched the city grow and grow. I am in a Children's Home and I enjoy living in it with having such a good corporation. *B.D.*

Nottingham today is rather dull and drab. The city centre leaves a lot to be desired, the buildings are old, some have been standing for one hundred years or more. Nottingham city centre should be developed on the lines of Coventry. There they have bright office blocks and brightly coloured shops but there is not much of that in Nottingham. Coventry city centre was heavily bombed during the war and for that reason all

CLIFFORD LEE extracted these comments on the city from unprepared essays by 14-year-olds at a Nottingham secondary modern school.

the new buildings have sprung up. Nottingham was not heavily bombed so the old buildings remain. I think the city council have old fashioned ideas. *J.R.*

Our school is one of the worst equipped in Nottingham and I think is one of the very few schools which is on two sites. There are no showers after P.E., the toilets freeze up in the winter because they are outdoors, the cycle sheds are just old air raid shelters, and there are not enough teachers for us. *I.G.*

Numerous people, when they leave an old Nottingham School building, enter an old factory building, in the centre of the industrial quarter . . . it is plain to see that Nottingham is overcrowded, underhoused and unfit for much of the rising generation. *P.E.*

I could name at least six pieces of waste land which would be used for building. *A.C.*

We wouldn't mind a few more ice stadiums. *T.J.*

The only interesting thing about Nottingham his the castle. *E.S.*

On the land outside the castle there is a Robin Hood statue, half of him vandalised. *R.B.*

I think they should have more amusements in the way of one arm bandits. *P.K.*

Nottingham is a city of supermarkets. *R.B.*

Nottingham has got too many black people. *A.K.*

. . . some of the black people are very polite and better than the English. *S.C.*

Many coloured people live in Nottingham of which many work on the buses. A lot of these people are attacked coming home from work. I think these people deserve protection. I am glad to see that Nottingham firms give coloured people jobs instead of persecuting like other town counsels. *C.N.*

The police could be a bit more polite. *R.F.*

The people who Design the layouts for the roads and trafick island want shooting because it's money whasted. *A.K.*

Today the slums are still being demolished and the factories are becoming more and more. *J.P.*

Riotous Times in Nottingham 1754-1854

A RIOTOUS TIME: NOTTINGHAM 1754-1854.

"as poor as a stockinger"—OLD EXPRESSION.

"For the last quarter of the century troops were an almost permanent feature of the scene. Contingents of the Oxford Blues and of Light Dragoons were quartered in the town and in 1792 a barracks was built in the park. Two years later (1794) the South Nottinghamshire Yeomanry came into being. Primarily the regiment was part of the general defence preparations being made against a possible French invasion, but it also provided a safeguard against the disturbed internal state of the country, and, as its early history shows, it was in fact largely used for police work of this kind throughout the long war with France. There were times in these iron years when Nottingham presented something of the aspect of an occupied town."

A HISTORY OF NOTTINGHAMSHIRE—*A. C. Wood.*

1754, election riots; 1755, bread prices riot; 1766, cheese prices riot (cheeses were snatched from the stalls at the Goose Fair and were hurled or rolled about, one bowling over the Mayor when he tried to intervene. Troops were called out.); 1779, riot following defeat of an Act to regulate prices and conditions in the framework-knitting trade (the Riot Act was read, 300 special constables were enrolled and cavalry was brought in. The Associated Stockingers was suppressed and its papers were seized.); 1783, riot about prices for work (troops brought in); 1795, disturbance about the price of butter; 1787, riot about conditions in the trade with the first framebreaking (an Act was passed making framebreaking a felony punishable by transportation for from seven to fourteen years: but an agreement on wages and prices was secured); 1788, meat prices riot (the Shambles was wrecked and the doors of the stalls were taken off and burned in the Market Place); 1790, election riot (troops called) and trade prices riot; 1791, trade prices riot; 1792, meat prices riot (doors of stalls again burned); 1793, conservative counter-revolutionary riots following the declaration of war—supporters of the French Revolution were attacked and an effigy of Tom Paine was burned in the Market Place; 1794, further political disturbances; 1795, riots about election results and about bread and meat prices; 1796, political disturbances; 1799, food prices riot (one witness stated that in 17 years residence in the town he had seen 17 major riots); 1800, bread riots.

1811, Luddite activities (a large-scale outburst of framebreaking. Police from Bow Street were brought to Nottingham and nine troops of horse and two regiments of infantry were brought into the Midlands. A Bill was passed the following year making framebreaking punishable by death. One of the few who violently resisted it in the House of Lords was Byron, who had close associations with the district. He said: "I have traversed the seat of war in the peninsula. I have been in some of the most oppressed provinces of Turkey, but never under the most despotic of infidel governments have I beheld such squalid wretchedness as I have seen since my return in the heart of a Christian country."); 1814-1820, framebreaking (—an early example of direct action. Wood says, In 1819 many of the stockingers who worked in their own homes brought in their frames and stacked them at the hosiers' doors, blocking the streets.).

1831, the Reform Riot. The Bill was rejected by the Lords at 6 a.m. on Saturday, October 8th. A few in the city had the news that evening but it was not generally known until the mail-coach arrived on Sunday morning. Rumours of rioting in Derby filtered in and the town was crowded for the Goose Fair. The Mayor received 19 separate requests to convene a meeting and stone-throwing at the windows of anti-reformers began. The crowds were dispersed by the 15th Hussars. On the Monday a meeting of some 20,000 suporters of the reform movement passed without incident but in the afternoon a windmill belonging to an anti-reformer was destroyed and the mob learnt that some of the troops had been sent to Derby. Colwick Hall, home of an opponent of the bill, was pillaged (Mary Musters, Byron's first love, had to hide in the shrubbery) and an unsuccessful attempt to storm the House of Correction in order to release the prisoners took place. A part of the mob then broke away and forced open the castle gates. Tapestries were cut into squares and sold to bystanders and the building was fired and completely gutted. On the Tuesday a silk mill at Beeston was fired—three of the ringleaders were hanged later—and there was an unsuccessful attempt to enter Wollaton Hall. But the troops had now been greatly strengthened and after further skirmishing the town was cleared. The message of the riot, together with the one at Bristol and smaller disturbances throughout the country, was received and understood. The Reform Bill was hastily passed without serious opposition the following summer.

1839, Chartist agitation and demonstration. Troops brought in. 1854, bread riots.

"It is only by making the ruling few uneasy that the oppressed many can obtain a particle of relief."—JEREMY BENTHAM.

Nottingham Mutual Aid
Shop stewards at Raleigh Industries last winter arranged for the "adoption" by 9,000 trade unionists of an orphaned Nottingham family of nine.

Nottingham Priorities
According to a survey financed by an anonymous group of professional people in Nottingham the principal topics of political interest for Nottingham's citizens are (in this order) old age pensions, roads, capital punishment, and nuclear disarmament.

Nottingham Prisoners
A group of prisoners serving preventive detention sentences at Nottingham Prison wrote last autumn to the Prison Reform Council and MPs, declaring that the extension of the pre-release hostel scheme to PD prisoners recommended as an interim measure pending abolition of preventive detention by the Advisory Council on the Treatment of Offenders, was being operated unfairly, causing "a general atmosphere of tension."

Planning for Man and Motor IN NOTTINGHAM

Paul Ritter

THE NOTION THAT MOTORS AND MEN SHOULD MOVE along separate lines came surprisingly slowly to the descendents of those who witnessed the strict separation of the railways. And they were less busy and less dangerous than roads. Clarence Stein, Lewis Mumford and others thought logically on the subject as long ago as the mid-twenties, when the traffic problems in the U.S.A. were approximately those that face us now, here in Britain. Radburn was the first town projected, with a system of paths quite separate from its roads, and both leading to each house but on opposite sides. Radburn has given its name to the system of traffic segregation that relies on horizontal separation. In central areas and expensive sites it is often logical to segregate vertically, placing one or other traffic above.

Although safety seems the most dramatic advantage of walking and driving well apart, this is a negative outlook. The positive advantages of a walk-way system, with its clean air, lack of loud noise, its proper human scale, enclosure and social amenities, connecting directly to schools, shops, pubs, parks, stations, etc., quite apart from safety, make it the only rational way of planning. From the driver's point of view, there is more efficiency and greater pleasure in driving. Studies have shown that, economically, this system compares favourably with the most economic other types of layout; that sociologically, more friend-liness and co-operation is found along paths; and, aesthetically, archi-tects and planners can practice the true, fine art of the profession; when building to a proper scale in the realm of the car, and more important, in the areas where man is supreme. It is impossible to design success-fully to one scale only and that dominated by the demands of the vehicle.

In describing the various applications of the basic idea to Notting-ham, it will be useful to look individually at (a) new housing, (b) inter-war housing in need of regeneration, (c) urban renewal in terms of the

PAUL RITTER was born in 1925 and now lives in Nottingham where he practices as a planning consultant and lectures at the School of Architecture. He and his wife Jean wrote The Free Family, *and his children wrote* Everybody Silly Sometimes. *He organised the "Child's Eye View" exhibition and the much-travelled "Man and Motor" exhibition. His newly published book* Man and Motor *is an essential companion volume to the Buchanan report.*

city as a whole, (d) and the city centre itself.

(a) New Housing

It is likely that any new housing planned by the City of Nottingham will be of the Radburn type. Indeed a small scheme of that nature was planned for Basford in 1961, not too early, considering the fact that Nottingham has been a study and propaganda centre of the idea since 1952. Not only little bits but every area of new housing must have traffic segregation at its roots. The stark, bitter tragedy of the Clifton estate may be modified, even now, but this sort of thing must never be repeated, not even in tiny schemes. Beeston has shown the way, not only to Nottingham, but the world. It became the first council to pass a resolution that all its future housing should be of this nature. One only hopes that this ruling is enforced on the private developer as well as on the council estates. The spectacular advantages of such a layout, with a properly inserted under-pass for pedestrians, linking all people to the shops and to the recreation grounds without the need to cross a single road, and conveniently, are shown in the scheme for the Ilkeston Road Estate, where 500 houses are to be laid out in that manner. Architects in Nottingham have been in the forefront in persuading private developers to experiment with traffic segregation. Accidents at Clifton and their publicity have made the people of Nottingham as ready as any to welcome the overdue introduction of ideas that lead to a better, safer, more beautiful environment, and, what is more, with economy.

(b) Regeneration of Housing built between the Wars

Such housing will be structurally sound for a long time. It is important not to neglect these areas and indeed research has shown how comparatively cheap and easy it is to do something about them. The missing amenities are: play spaces, particularly for the young, as the older ones can ride their bicycles to the nearest recreation ground; garages and parking spaces; old people's dwellings (at the moment old people, shrunken families, have to leave the area they have lived in so long or have many empty rooms, as too many dwellings are three bedroom houses); and smaller gardens, particularly in some places, where the traditional lay-out has left immense areas to the embarrassment of many a tenant. On top of these felt and recognised needs which can be derived from any survey, there are those subtle but great improvements which the fine art of town planning can bring: the delightful small scale environment of a separate footpath system to bus stops and shops and schools or just for a walk. Many through roads, which are dangerous can be made into cul-de-sacs without harm or inconvenience.

All this sort of thing has been illustrated on a design study of Aspley estate. It is important to stress that, with the scarcity and high price of land, it is a great asset to find sites for two extra dwellings an acre and one garage for every ten houses and play spaces, from existing road space and gardens which are too large. These assets must be balanced against the cost of providing the extra lighting and surfacing to the paths. The alternative way of providing garages for example, which the City of Nottingham has chosen, i.e. spoiling the few bits of open ground left in such estates, is leading to a piece-meal, uneconomic way of dealing with the problem as a whole.

(c) Urban Renewal in General

Exceptionally dense housing clustered around a very concentrated town centre will have to be replaced within the next few years. A bad start has been made at Sneinton and in the Alfreton Road—Ilkeston Road wedge. The shops and the pedestrians should have been taken out of such nerve-racking death traps as Alfreton Road and St. Ann's Well Road. This can be done effectively when whole wedges are comprehensively developed, as is the rule in most cities now. Taking a wedge between two roads, the shops and path system are planned within it, and the service and motor traffic on the outside. The footpaths then form an effective and attractive way of getting into town, which is the accepted way for many workers in the city. Indeed some schemes for Nottingham do already hint at this type of development but it is essential that it should become a general principle so that a path system throughout the whole town is created. In Nottingham we are fortunate that the bones of such a system already exist, much of it as a ring which would link the path spines of the wedges. Underpasses become worthwhile and essential once large pedestrian flow is directed into attractive, convenient channels. Most urgent is perhaps the one at the north-west corner of the Forest; here a very large comprehensive development is scheduled with a pedestrian interior, a path system linking schools, shops and all the inhabitants to the Forest adjoining this area corner to corner. But there is no underpass planned at that point, a monstrous omission, a fiendishly designed trap to catch the children impatiently running to their play and to stop those whose mothers are worried about getting across Gregory Boulevard safely. If the municipality does not propose this underpass then there is no better point of application for the Nottingham Civic Society than to press for this measure or even collect money towards it.

A comprehensive footpath network ought to be part of the development plan of ever town. In Nottingham the Tunnel from the Park to Derby Road is an immensely valuable asset, now totally ignored but of vital importance once the Park is comprehensively developed, as it surely must be, taking as an example the Calthorpe Estate redevelopment at Birmingham. In other words private developers, if they wish to avoid being taken over by the compulsory purchase orders of land hungry cities such as Birmingham or Nottingham, will have to develop comprehensively themselves.

We must avoid such stupid situations as the one at present concerning the Arboretum: The Nottingham Girls High School has an exit to the Arboretum and via a Victorian and excellent underpass this leads on one side, almost directly to Mansfield Road, and on the other, to Waverley Street, or Goldsmith Street and Town. However, in the winter darkness, lack of lamps in the park and lack of protection makes this route a forbidden one, leaving the children to the more frequent but less publicised danger of motor traffic.

To summarise, urban renewal means amongst other things the

gradual establishment of a city-wide footpath network. What happens to the footpath system when it gets into the centre is the next point.

(d) Central Development and Renewal

Several ways of segregating traffic in the centre of Nottingham are applicable, both ultimately, and in sequence, as the stages of re-development proceed. The simplest and obvious first step, already taken by many towns in Germany and some in Scandinavia, and resulting in better trade, is to close to motor traffic some of the streets for a few hours of the day, say from 11 a.m. to 5 p.m., delivery and servicing taking place during the remaining hours. This change cost nothing at all. As parking is usually forbidden in such streets neither the motorist shopper, nor the shopkeeper have anything to lose as they walk from a parking space to the shop. Clumber Street and Pelham Street are such roads in Nottingham: their intimacy and delight would once again be appreciated if one could walk in the middle of the road, stroll along, looking first right then left into all the shops; cross without danger and even take children along without fear and without the incessant clinging to hands and skirts which now makes shopping a doubtful pleasure (or sheer misery, for the mother. This idea could, should, and I hope will, be tried tomorrow.

The second technique of making the city centre a welcoming, relaxing, gay place is to close some streets permanently to traffic and resurface and furnish them so that, although the fire brigade, etc., can drive in for any emergency, the black asphalt is replaced by paving and patterns, right for the eye and the scale of the pedestrian. In such cases it is essential to provide adequate service access at the back of the shops. A pedestrian dominated space would make the vehicle take care, as in for example, the Arboretum at the moment. Again, shopkeepers who for years have thought this sort of thing would make their sales drop have realised from foreign examples that the reverse takes place. In Gothenburg the authorities were embarrassed in that neighbouring streets of shops asked to be closed to traffic after the first example was an overwhelming success. And in Gothenburg no extra parking was provided. If in Nottingham the extra provision of parking went hand in hand with the closing to traffic of streets (and the smoother flow of traffic and public transport besides) then shopkeepers have much to gain.

The third way of developing the centre in a rational way is to use space at a number of levels. It has been found in Chester for centuries that shopping on two levels can pay. But the attempt to introduce this in Coventry failed to some extent. Research has shown that people will use upper level shopping if they are led naturally and gradually onto it. Taking Parliament Street as a starting point, Nottingham provides a fine opportunity to channel people onto an upper shopping deck on the North side of the Old Market Square by starting such paths along Market Street and Queen Street. In that manner extra " frontage " is gained for no land costs and with very low constructional costs. From the other side, Wheeler Gate and St. Peter's Walk, the lower level can be exploited and the entire Old Market Square could once again fulfil a " market " function on a level slightly lower than its present one, leaving an open square above to fulfil the need for an open space. Planned or not planned, the city changes radically. We have learned a little about the skills of city planning and must obviously guide the developments of the next 50 or 100 years, realising how much more rapid and drastic changes are likely to be.

Can we plan so far ahead when things are changing at this rate ? The question is answered by the constancy of certain values in human life. Just as privacy will always be a need, so indeed is getting together. It has been shown that getting together is most efficient and pleasant on foot, as indeed shopping is one way of getting together. Similarly, wheel plus motor, are inventions that we are not likely ever to give up, except perhaps to hover over similar surfaces now used by wheels. Thus the need for segregation, whatever motor or propulsion, remains a constant need. On the other hand the use of cars, particularly in countries outside the USA, is growing rapidly. The provision of parking in town centres and of car provision in residential areas has to increase, and with it the use of public transport. It is quite impracticable and inadvisable, except for small new towns, to attempt a provision for 100% car usage of all inhabitants in the centre. It is silly to use private cars to go the same distance day in day out. Better public transport is the obvious answer.

Town planners are slowly learning that in each old town, sooner or later a value judgment will have to be made: how many private cars do we allow ? There is no other way. (Even if that decision is not made explicitly it is still made implicitly as there just is not the space to provide roads for the cars that all people would like to bring into the centre.) The pedestrian system with its square and precincts and alleys, then achieves the human scale, the pulsating system in the centre, free of traffic. If the human scale is right, there is no danger that life and bustle will disappear with the cars. One visit to the Central Market or Sneinton Market will convince anyone in a twinkle that here is life.

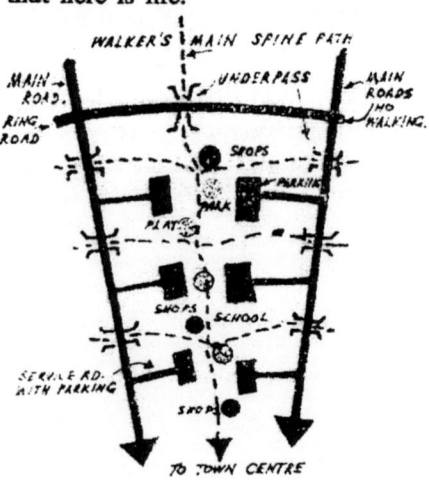

"Taking a wedge between two roads, the shops and path system are planned within it, and the service and motor traffic on the outside. The footpaths then form an effective and attractive way of getting into town, which is the accepted way for many workers in the city."

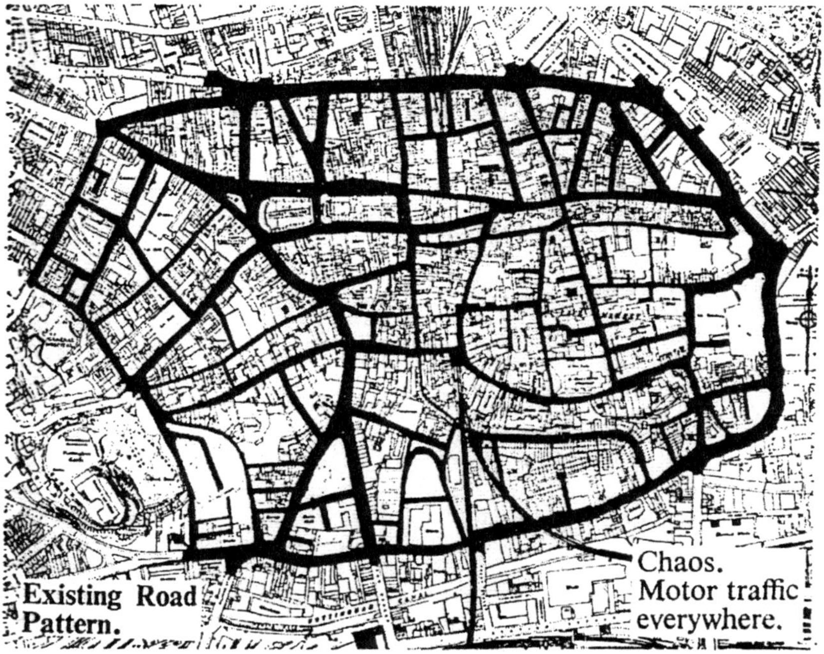

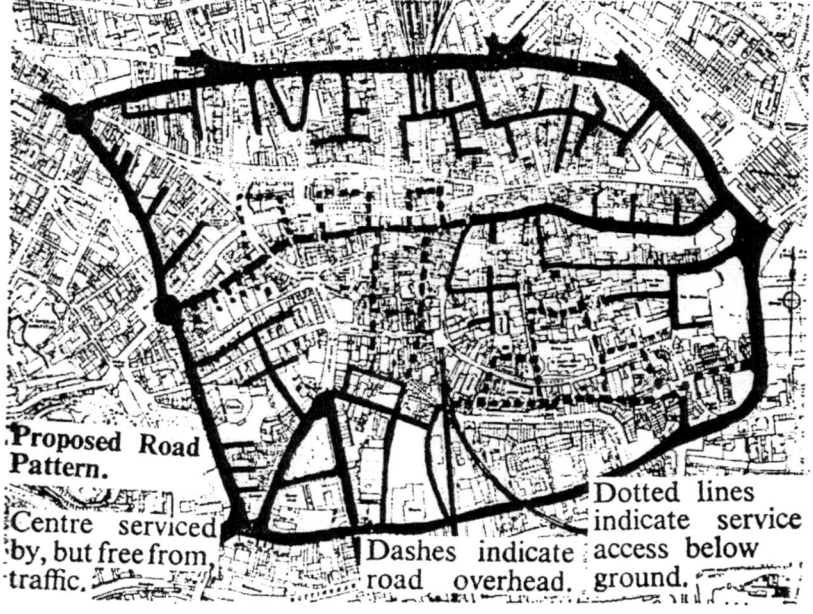

Existing Road Pattern.

Chaos. Motor traffic everywhere.

Proposed Road Pattern.

Centre serviced by, but free from, traffic.

Dashes indicate road overhead.

Dotted lines indicate service access below ground.

PAGES FROM A NOTTINGHAM NOTEBOOK
HAROLD DRASDO

GEORGE ORWELL REMARKS SOMEWHERE THAT WEAPONS DEMONSTRATE the characters as well as the technologies of their makers: the nuclear bomb, he says, fits the totalitarian state; the selective longbow might be a libertarian weapon. Certainly it was in the name of liberty that Robin Hood annoyed the keepers of Nottingham Castle. But that legendary figure, his exploits recounted all over England by the time of Richard II, was a dangerous hero for the common people and in the later tales the Establishment subdued him with a knighthood. If you can't beat them, buy them.

Three hundred years later, Nottingham saw in reality an act of sabotage provoked by the threat of a more significant betrayal. The Civil War began in August 1642 when the king raised his standard here and called his supporters to arms. Locally there was no enthusiasm, the standard ominously blew down, and he moved away; in fact the town was held by the Roundheads throughout the war. But, the new society achieved, some of those who had fought for it did not care much for the form they saw it taking. The resourceful Colonel Hutchinson (one of the Regicides—he died in imprisonment in Sandown Castle) distrusting Cromwell's " poisonous ambition " secretly procured an order from the Council of State for the demolition of the castle. The Commonwealth would need no fortesses, he assured Cromwell, when the latter learnt of its destruction. But the Lord Protector was furious: it seems he liked castles; he could have found a use for it still.

Castles sprang up again like leaders. Within thirty years a new building, less military in style, had been raised on the same site. It stood through the stormy years of rioting for food and work which culminated in the Luddite troubles; until, in 1831, the property then of the notorious fourth Duke of Newcastle, it was sacked and burned by the desperate populace when the news of the defeat of the Reform Bill reached the city.

But even this was not the end. Another castle dominates the city today, a symbol, if you like, of the protean shapes of authority. For, very appropriately, it serves now as an art gallery and museum as if to exhibit the extent of the state's claims; to bear witness to the fact that the art of government includes the government of art; to remind men of the municipality's involvement in every province of their lives— taking their taxes and caring for their aesthetic appetites not simply with its selection of paintings but also with its Watch Committee.

HAROLD DRASDO, who lives in Nottingham and teaches English, was born in Bradford in 1930. He has contributed to several issues of ANARCHY *and wrote the latest guide to Lakeland rock-climbs.*

How deep does this interference go? And how effective is it? What chance is there, in a fairly typical provincial city, of access to radical ideas in politics or to new disturbances in the arts? . . . Well, here are a couple of scenes from provincial life. Firstly, the browsers in Nottingham City Library roused by the unnecessarily loud voice of a young librarian: ",Yes, sir, we have a copy of *Tropic of Cancer* but it's not kept on the shelves. It's in the reference section. You can look at it there if you want to." The poor, sick, shabby old man did not like the attention his enquiry had won him. He crept out whilst the decent citizens watched him with amusement or distaste . . . From public service to private society. The Film Study Group of the Co-operative Film Society saw Jean Vigo's *Zéro de Conduite* and discussed censorship afterwards. The speakers congratulated themselves on British liberty and mentioned their pleasure at having seen Vigo's classic without interference. But the words that the sub-title said to the headmaster in English did not adequately represent the words that Tabard said to him in French. " Je vous dis merde! "—the very expression which was one of the roots of the film to the director, whose father had used it to headline a celebrated article in *La Guerre Sociale* and had subsequently spent two years in prison for his polemics. A trivial point, perhaps? To me it seemed to help bury the bitter actualities behind the film, half-buried already by time, apathy and ignorance.

These two incidents pertain exactly to the two sorts of cultural enterprises which the city offers. Scanning briefly the public or commercial facilities there are seven cinemas in the city centre and as many again within two or three miles. There is the New Playhouse, open since December but with a history that would fill a book; it's not possible to describe it or evoke its atmosphere in a few words: it promises well for the future, the actors having already had a fracas with the city elders at a reception in the Council House. It isn't likely that this excitement will upset the Theatre Royal or affect it even remotely. Further, the city is provided with an impressive central library (I haven't yet asked if a list of unshelved objectionable fiction is issued with the other subject lists); an incomparable bookshop (there is no serious competitor with which to compare it) having five departments and a staff of more than a hundred; three art galleries; the Albert Hall.

To supplement our fixed assets we have the occasional cultural windfall. Centre 42 passed through some time ago, selling a fraction of its eight thousand poundsworth of entertainment: plays, exhibitions, folksong, jazz. Christopher Logue, with a fetching bravado, read his poems to the Raleigh workers in their own canteen. On the subject of poetry it is interesting to see the audiences John Neville's jazz and poetry sessions draw. The enthusiasm is astonishing. All these young people who have learnt somewhere (where?) that all this Kenneth Patchen is the right thing: they're not sure where it's leading but they're determined to be sent. Perhaps, though, it is Neville's person rather than Patchen's poetry that attracts them. Any kind of musical event is well patronised. The Sadlers Wells production of *Peter Grimes* gave immense pleasure and CND's Remembrance Day folksong concert brought in a surprisingly large audience.

In an ambivalent position, offering lectures to the public but built by isolationists, there is the university. Culture has roots in cash, said Lawrence, and this institution sprang " out of the noble loot/ derived from shrewd cash-chemistry/ by good Sir Jesse Boot." From the north-east the pedestrian reaches the main buildings through pleasant rolling parkland but he will be soaked to the skin if it's raining. On the south, the shortest approach by public transport, these buildings are defended by an ornamental lake into which, on the darkest winter nights, strangers attempting to take the obvious short-cut are said occasionally to plunge.

These are the public enterprises. But, on reflection, it is clear that the dedication of a quite small number of people provides amenities of almost equal significance; through the agency, I mean, of various amateur groups. The prop for most of these is the Co-operative Society with its excellent Arts Theatre and Educational Centre. The Arts Theatre's productions appeal to a very wide audience and include popular comedy, opera, and occasional revues or musicals as well as serious drama; in addition to the dramatic group they have an orchestra, a choral and operatic group, a tape recording club, junior groups, and so on—sometimes they work in liaison. I've mentioned the film society already. If you attend regularly the annual subscription gives you each showing at less than two shillings. For this you see, together with interesting supporting features, the classics you've missed. The level is that of similar societies all over Britain and programmes during the last two years have presented *Les Jeux Interdits, The Red Badge of Courage* and *La Notte;* on occasion there is something really startling and unexpected—Kobayashi's *No Greater Love* shook me. Regrettably, the special film series has collapsed; the really seminal films draw about thirty from a population of 300,000.

The most ambitious of all the purely amateur ventures seems to be the Nottingham Theatre Club. Here are some of its productions of the last three seasons: Durrenmatt's *The Visit;* Euripides' *The Bacchae;* Donleavy's *The Ginger Man;* O'Neill's *Long Day's Journey into Night;* Max Frisch's *The Fire Raisers;* Arnold Wesker's *I'm Talking About Jerusalem;* Webster's *The Duchess of Malfi;* Ibsen's *Pillars of Society;* Brecht's *Chalk Circle.* And all these splendidly produced and well attended. No compromise and nothing provincial about this selection; these plays may be of unequal status but taken as a whole they make no slanted statement about the condition of man. They reflect the club's admirable policy: to show plays not previously performed in the city; to pay attention to unusual or experimental drama; to remember the classical drama as a standard. The O'Neill play was, remarkably, the first amateur performance in England; and all of John Whiting's plays except his last had their first provincial performances here. What more can one ask ? Certainly, a part of our cultural freedom comes to us through those who shape the enduring traditions of groups like this.

Considering all this activity it can hardly be said that the cinema or theatregoer is badly served here. What about the man who wants to read? Obviously, his first task is to penetrate the thought barrier of the mass media. Look at the national press: coerced by the pressures of advertisers; always forced into gestures in order to maintain or increase sales; always aggregating, the controlling groups becoming more and more powerful, less and less in number; obliged to inflate or exclude items of news to make so many pages of print; squeezing out minority opinion; gagged by the seventeen D notices standing at this moment; provided with a lower stratum so exuberantly irresponsible that it serves excellently to make the " quality " press appear, by contrast, as sufficiently serious and disinterested. These tendencies and forces serve different ends and sometimes negate each other. But, in general, public opinion is so conditioned that there is rarely a need to create specific defences against revolutionary ideas; they are burned out like meteorites entering the atmosphere.

Reading, in fact, can be quite expensive. If, to take the nearest instance, you are developing an interest in libertarian ideas, you will find little available in the city periodical form. You must get what you want by subscription and you will spend time in learning slowly what is currently published. Your initial access to this literature is probably, in any case, by chance; not many copies of *Anarchy* reach Nottingham; does anyone here read *Liberation* or *Dissent* ? The same is true of literary magazines. In London you will see how much doesn't arrive in the Midlands. (You must go to Paris to find the books that only pass Dover in hiding.) The difficulties are caused by the fact that reading is a solitary activity and the reader need not necessarily co-operate with his fellows. But clearly there is a place here for mutual aid. Private film societies and dramatic groups are free, in the first instance, of the restrictions of censorship. A co-operative library takes a small step in this direction in that jointly members can afford to buy books which have not been proceeded against because they are priced for protection. No-one wishes to own all the journals and books which he would like to glance through but which the public library cannot manage to cover for reasons of finance or space, or which it must conceal so as not to incur the displeasure of certain powerful gangs. Before the enactment of the first public libraries legislation, industrial centres like Nottingham had a variety of reading societies and mechanics' and artisans' libraries; even today small groups of people sharing the same interest co-operate in this way naturally; but it is the individuals who are outside these groups and who are groping for information alone and uncertainly who need these services. At present, an interest in libertarian ideas takes men haphazardly, stirred by impulses of attraction or repulsion towards aspects of modern political and social life or towards events or gestures in history or literature. We must try to advertise our belief in a coherent ideological position at the intersection of the lines of thought to which these impulses give rise.

Of course, a co-operative library might go further than this to end its literary malnutrition and here the Watch Committee jerks itself awake. But this operates both ways the Watch Committee ought to engage our attention too. Individually, we learn so little about it without tedious and time-consuming research. Some of its decisions are, it is true, easily accessible in the monthly Civic News. It records refusals of permission for the screening of films without always naming the films concerned. It sends some of its members on BBFC courses of censorship—what do they tell them there ? It blandly approves a proposal " to construct a Civil Defence sub-Area Control Centre *underneath* the proposed new Police Station at Church Lane, Bulwell. . . ." (Italics mine; an expensive alteration). It considers items " which must of necessity be dealt with in confidence." It performs, also, a host of socially essential tasks and there's the rub. We get these services in a package deal with no provision for opting out. It is a model of the national situation. We pay for hospitals, schools and better roads and learn later that our enterprising representatives have bought us a few shares in hydrogen bombs too, whether we will or no.

Nottingham's Watch Committee is not, as far as I know, one of the really paranoic ones. If it has shown any signs of prurience or imbecility like that of Bradford's some months ago, I have missed them. We do not resist it solely because it might meddle with something of great literary or artistic merit for we know very well that most of the items it might object to are contemptible or unpleasant: it challenges us simply, as Everest challenged Mallory, " because it is there." We know that the end of censorship must lead, in the context of our economy, to a flood of rubbish—one of the component awareneses of our censorship is the knowledge that the profit-motive makes men bad—but this would still be less disgusting than the existence of censorship. For myself, I can manage without it; it would be impertinent of me to recommend it for anyone else.

Actually, the question is broader than this. The edges of what we are allowed to know are of the utmost significance. (Wittgenstein : " the limits of my language mean the limits of my world.") No man, anywhere, can validly generalise about government or culture without making the test of logic : he must examine what he is permitted to know in comparison with what he is forbidden to read or discover. The first article of the Manifesto for the Flagless Man says—read anything you like : any government, party, religion, philosophy, group or person obstructing you must be resisted in proportion to the power exercised. And the academic question of a world without censorship? Attention would have to be directed on to two teaching topics : the recognition of the portentous gap between word and act, idea and reality; and the clear definition of personal responsibility in every imaginable situation.

Perhaps, for every Watch Committee we ought to have a Counterwatch Group, excluding those with political affiliations, having the function of observing and investigating the Committee's more undemocratic activities. A Counterwatch Club, if you like, offering the services of mutual assistance already suggested and serving as a focus for libertarian ideas and activities. Here is my copy of the *Kama Kala*, a handsome volume of Indian erotic sculpture, price £7 17s. 6d. and worth at least five shillings; it ought to be out as a paperback but the law might not like it; let me know if you would like to borrow it. Shall we hold a Counterwatch Week ? Produce a booklet with a wide selection of good unexceptionable passages from banned books, simply to remind men that more English has been written than has been published in England ? It might be possible to stage an exhibition of items which have been ruled not permissible at different places in Britain in the Welfare State era, crediting each piece with place, date and available reasons, and staging the whole without risk to the sponsors by blacking out the relevant passages in books, clothing tastefully any statutory likely to offend and so forth. The exhibition might travel the country whilst different groups examined the responses of their moral guardians. It is a pity that the emancipated man expresses himself so seldom. The Home Office apologised recently to Queen Frederica of Greece and to the Cuban Ambassador for its lack of control over its subjects. Did any of us think to apologise to Lenny Bruce for our lack of control over the Home Office ? That would have been a gracious gesture and William Ayscough might have made it. Nottingham's first printer, he was not, it would seem, a man who would have consorted well with our servile generation. His wife shared his radical opinions and she carried on his business after his death; we find her in 1728 in the *Records of the Borough of Nottingham* summoned " ffor printing and publishing Severall Scandalous and indecent expressions . . . tending to bring the Kings Ministers of State into contempt."

But perhaps this article has become too strident in tone and considers the amenities of the city in too narrow a sense. We have a lot of bingo here. Discussing Eliot's *Notes Toward the Definition of Culture* several years ago in the *Kenyon Review*, an American critic said: " Anyone who wants to meditate about the history of culture would do well to walk any afternoon in the vicinity of Times Square. Where do all these crowds come from ? How do they fill their day ? What is to be done with them?" You might ask these questions in Nottingham of an evening. A lively city with its people conspicuously bent on pleasure. See them in Slab Square on Saturday night, magnificent little girls and carefree young men, the creatures of Alan Sillitoe-land : Stiletto-land, you may think, considering the well-heeled young women and the knifing posters with which the police have decorated the pubs. Before the drinking starts the crowds wander about the speakers in the square, reminding you of Chesterton's Englishmen : " and some men talked of freedom / But England talked of ale." Admittedly, the pubs *are* the best in England; I feel a rich sense of tradition in drinking in " The Trip to Jerusalem " (cut into the base of the solid rock on which the Castle stands) and reflecting on the eight centuries of drinkers who have preceded me, back to the men impressed into the Crusades. But at the end of the evening there is an element amongst the crowds of which no city might be proud. Have there been many strikes like our busmen's walkout last year?—a protest at repeated assaults upon conductors on the late night buses. Is it for these young people that we demand more freedom ? Possibly, we have to say: it is for anyone who wants it. They didn't, in any case, get these ideas from Lawrence or Nabokov or Miller—not even from *Der Spiegel* or the Spies for Peace. This sort of behaviour is taught nowhere in the pages which caused such storms. They learnt it somehow from the newspapers and from the pressures of the incompletely affluent society: they are depraved already, although, perhaps, they hardly read books at all.

"What *is* to be done with them ? " One direct answer was given by another American, Paul Goodman, writing in a recent issue of this journal about the more serious delinquency problems of New York. " The cure for their violent sexuality is to allow them guiltless sex. The cure for their defiance is to teach them their real enemies to fight. The cure for their foolish activism is to provide them with a world that has worthwhile tasks." And how are we to recognise these unspecified enemies ? someone may ask; isn't this the thing on which men can never agree ? . . . . If attention is paid to the first and last of Goodman's recommendations the enemies will identify themselves. Behind every juvenile delinquent stand the forces of senile delinquency.

I ONCE KNEW AN AMERICAN WRITER IN MAJORCA who, over a bottle of gin and a dish of spiced snails, smoking a two-peseta cigar, would lean back contentedly in his chair after finishing his work in the evening, and exclaim: " Ah! I wonder what the poor are doing tonight?" I didn't try to tell him, because I was poor myself. In any case, he didn't really want to know, because he was joking, and because he also had been poor.

In England there are half a million people out of work, and ten times that number living in real poverty, what I would call below the telly-line, as well as below the bread-line. The gap between the very poor and the normal rich is wider than it has even been. The adults of these five or six million people form part of those twenty-three per cent who regularly never bother to vote at a general election.

Voting can never make any difference to their plight. It would

---

ALAN SILLITOE, born in Nottingham 1928, started work at Raleigh's cycle factory 1942. He is the author of Saturday Night and Sunday Morning *1958,* The Loneliness of the Long-Distance Runner *1959,* The General *1960,* The Rats *1960,* Key to the Door *1961, and* The Ragman's Daughter *1963. David Brett's stage adaptation of his first book opens at the Nottingham Playhouse this month.*

take too long. They want to get out of it now, this minute, this week at the most. When you live from day to day, how can you believe anyone who says he will alter things in a few years ? The years ahead are an empty desert, without landmarks of any kind, beyond the imagination. Poor people live in the present.

The poor lack manoeuverability. Without money you are born and die in the same place. To travel presents difficulties that are rarely overcome. You are tied at the ankle, and cannot stray beyond a certain distance from the roots of your poverty. The advantage of this is that you become familiar with the environs of your sleeping place, and there may be a chance of living off the land.

Your world becomes small, intense and real. Your senses are sharpened but, strangely enough, this doesn't necessarily mean an increase in intelligence, or the ability to act. Intelligence is often stunted in the fight for order and food. A near-cretin, mustering energy in order to survive, may present a dextrous visage to the better-off, who imagine he must be cunning to survive at all on so little.

The very poor are too busy surviving to want to get on. To get on is something often dinned into them, handed down by the culture beneath which they exist. They are unable to take advantage of it, for to reach next week with clothes on your back, food still on the table, and enough life in your brain to face another week is the most they can do.

The rich, or normally well-off, cannot imagine how much an achievement this in fact is. The rich can accuse them of fecklessness, lack of thrift (qualities that the rich dare not enjoy if they want to stay where they are) but the greatest virtue of the poor is that they have learned how to survive without disturbing the rich.

Apart from the natural failings found in people of any class, they are where they are because of the lack of opportunity to develop intelligence or learn skill. Their life is maintained by patience, tenacity, scepticism and pride. This quality of survival is one that the better-off have forgotten how to use because they do not need it any more: to keep what they already have demands a different mental process.

Films on the telly, or at the cinema, giving examples of people who, one way or another, got on through personal striving, are enjoyed for the story, but believed only as a fairy tale is. That, they say, is not for the likes of us. In a way they are right. The poor not only know their place (maddening as this may seem to many) but they will go on knowing it until they can get out of it on their own terms.

The poor live in isolation, unreachable by private benevolence, goodness of heart, or sound advice. Poverty is a disease, as incurable as cancer, incurable because the resources of the state are not made to do a great surgical operation.

How can one define a poor person ? When I had some money in my pocket I was walking down Holland Road and saw a grey-bearded man in absolute rags lying on a piece of wall. Rain was pouring down. I offered him some money, but he waved me angrily away. I should have known better. The poor either earn money, ask for it, or take it. They have a way of keeping their self-respect, in these forms of getting what they need.

There are degrees of being poor. The most common is that of the man who earns twelve pounds a week and has a couple of children. If he is living in London he may pay four pounds a week for a room, and his wife will be unable to go to work because the children can't be left alone. This is not usually regarded as poverty. In such a room you might find a telly or radio. The man will smoke cigarettes, go to the pictures now and again, drink a pint maybe—all in small degree, after his rations are secure, sometimes when they are not.

Orwell did his nut about the diet of the poor, in *The Road to Wigan Pier*. He would do it again if he were still alive. Not for them the simple wholesome stuff. Frozen-this and processed-that, tinned muck, loaves of sliced, wrapped, steambaked pap, margarine and turnip marmalade, tea, flaky pastries made with axle-grease and saccharine, meat like froken rope—is what keeps people pale and frantic, and just strong enough to work, or strong enough not to. The womb-sweets and womb-custard (as advertised on telly) keep them close to the umbilical cord of the " deeply satisfying ".

If a poor family doesn't throw some of its money away each week on fags and the pictures they may go under quicker than if they do. Their morale cracks, and they end up either in the poor-house or the looney bin. This is a reason for the so-called fecklessness of the poor: a visit to the pictures is often better than a hot dinner.

A poor family cannot always find a room to live in. They may be terrorised and thrown out by someone wanting vacant possession of a house in an area becoming fashionable. Sometimes my eye catches an ad in a newspaper, of a house for sale, and the tagged-on phrase " vacant possession if desired " makes me think of two hundred police and bailiffs ejecting a family recently in St. Stephen's Gardens at four-thirty in the morning after a ten-day siege. A poor person can never be sure, from one week to the next, where he will be living. He has mobility within a wall. To get beyond the wall, into the big wide world, he needs an entrance ticket. That means money, and he knows it. The poor live in a vicious circle, work hard, and pay out so much a week in order to live—an eternal HP so as to get the biggest Bingo prize of all at the end of sixty or seventy years: death in a fine coffin.

There are different kinds of poverty then. First is the never-ending sort, which collapses in death, a poverty in which you were born, and from which you were never able to move. Then there is the poverty of the young man, say, who is to become a writer or painter: poverty from choice. This can be awful and degrading but, whatever he may say, it is a lesser form of evil than poverty. It is a stage to something else. It has compensations.

There is the poverty of the man who has known better days, as they say. This is bad enough, but he knows it is not the only state of living. He knows also that there is a possibility of alteration. At least he has had better days.

The worst poverty of all is that which afflicts the man who is out of work for a long time, through no fault of his own. This is a destitution of the spirit as well as a destitution of material means—the man who wants work yet has to see his children never quite getting enough to eat, who knows that something could be done about his situation but is powerless to do anything on his own. Such a man becomes filled with bitterness.

The poor know of only two classes in society. Their sociology is much simplified. There are *them* and *us*. Them are those who tell you what to do, who drive a car, use a different accent, are buying a house in another district, deal in cheques and not money, pay your wages, collect rent and telly dues, stop for you now and again at pedestrian crossings, can't look you in the eye, read the news on wireless or television, hand you the dole or national assistance money; the shopkeeper, copper, schoolteacher, doctor, health visitor, the man wearing the white dog-collar. Them are those who robbed you of your innocence, live on your backs, buy the house from over your head, eat you up, or tread you down. Above all, the poor who are not crushed in spirit hate the climbers, the crawlers, the happy savers, the parsimonious and respectable—like poison.

When there is widespread poverty, people help each other in order to survive, but when poverty is patchy, uneven, and separated in its unevenness, they lose faith in unity. They acquire a sense of guilt, and this is worst of all because it is unnecessary, underserved, and undermines even further their self-respect.

It creates a good atmosphere though, as far as action from outside is concerned: the government can ignore it. When many other people appear to be OK and getting on then the poor can imagine it is their own fault that they are poor. This accretion of guilt far outweighs the encouragement they are supposed to get from seeing people less poor, whose example they are expected to follow because they somehow have managed to eke out a better form of living.

If a poor person slides his hand on to some counter and pulls down a bar of chocolate he is dragged into the court and made to pay a hundred times its value. This is the basis of all justice as they see it. Is there not, they might ask, enough for everybody if all food were to be shared out? Enough room for us all to live in? You have to go on working, of course, work until you drop (that's all right, you have to work, expect to) but isn't there an abundance that, if shared out, would be enough for us, for everyone? It takes them a long time to realise that, while there is enough for the poor, there would not be enough for the rich. Only those who win a football pool see that.

Their folk heroes are those who try, by brains and daring, to get some share of the rich man's loot. He is superior to those who get it on the pools, which means the falling in of mere luck. The idolisation of Robin Hood went out centuries ago. If it hadn't, would schoolbooks still tell of him? It never quite rings true to them that someone should, as an individual act, rob the rich and give to the poor. That was a way of buying off enough of the poor, who would prevent those not given anything going straight to the source of wealth—that only Robin could get at. Robin had an unofficial monopoly of wealth by being able forcibly to tax the rich. There is a saying: "Robin Hood? Robbin' bastard, more like." He ended up becoming one of the king's men.

The poor idolise and idealise those who bring off wage or train robberies and don't get caught. A patriotic Victoria Cross or George Medal has nothing on the thrill of reading about this. They don't expect any of the robbers' loot: the mere act of striking is enough for them.

A man who takes from those who have more than himself is not a robber. The word "robber" is applied in all its tragic depth only when one poor man robs another poor man. If the first factor of poverty is lack of mobility, the second is powerlessness. There is nothing you can do about it, except endure and survive. If you can't help yourself, then don't expect God to do so. If God helps those who help themselves, then how is it possible for him to be on anybody else's side but the rich? God is a Tory, a landlord, a millionaire, a magistrate. If he's a worker he's the sort of bastard who started out with five pounds and made five millions. He did it on his mates' backs, and wouldn't give them the skin off his nose.

For the desperate, which means those who feel their poverty most, and deserve it least (if such a thing can be said) there is always the gas oven. But that is your trump card, a fate you often think about in order to get yourself over the worst times.

If it is used it is only as a last desperate defence. It is the great individual act of which you are capable—without asking anybody's permission except that of your own deepest inner self. You don't sign for it, you do it of your own free will, to spite either someone you know, or the world in general, or because there is nothing else left to do but that—for a thousand reasons. It has a dignity nothing else has been able to give, and few are able to make this last act of dignity. It is the final freedom which no-one can take from you, which depends on you alone.

To me, after saying all this, the poor do not have a common psychology. That would be an inadmissable statement from a writer. They are all individuals for whom the rich—who form the state—are responsible. And because the rich can never effectively help the poor (they just don't want to know them) then the only solution is a political system which makes such responsibility not an act of charity but a fundamental principle.

Nottingham Babies

Research psychologists John and Elizabeth Newson report in *Infant Care in an Urban Community* (Allen and Unwin 42s.) how 700 Nottingham mothers of all social classes rear their babies, including the discrepancies between what mothers feel are the official answers and what they actually do. over such matters as feeding, pot-training, dummies, tantrums, "spoiling" and settling the children to sleep. Most are conscious of being more indulgent than their own parents, there is a "very widespread preference for indulgence rather than discipline." There are still many class differences: middle-class mothers smack their babies less, report fewer temper tantrums and are less inclined to punish them for playing with their genitals. In spite of all the propaganda for breast-feeding it is widely disliked: half the working-class babies are weaned from the breast in a month. Breasts are so eroticised today, the authors suggest, that mothers are shy of revealing them to their husband, to slightly older children, and even to baby.